Sound Effects Artist

ODD JOBS

VIRGINIA LOH-HAGAN

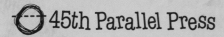 **45th Parallel Press**

Published in the United States of America by Cherry Lake Publishing
Ann Arbor, Michigan
www.cherrylakepublishing.com

Content Adviser: James Shin, motion picture creative, Sony Pictures Entertainment, Culver City, California
Reading Adviser: Marla Conn, ReadAbility, Inc.
Book Design: Felicia Macheske

Photo Credits: © Vancouver Film School / www.flickr.com / CC-BY-2.0, cover, 17, 29, 28; © Northfoto /
Shutterstock.com, 5, 11; © Fotokostic / Shutterstock.com; © ncognet0 / iStock, 8-9; © keith morris / Alamy, 13;
© Kzenon / Shutterstock.com, 14; © Master1305 / Shutterstock.com, 19; © Tony Bock / ZUMA Press / Newscom,
22; © wellphoto / Shutterstock.com, 23; © dragoncello / Dreamstime.com, 25; © Fotomicar / Shutterstock.
com, 27; © ARENA Creative / Shutterstock.com, cover and multiple interior pages; © oculo / Shutterstock.
com, multiple interior pages; © Denniro / Shutterstock.com, multiple interior pages; © PhotoHouse /
Shutterstock.com, multiple interior pages; © Miloje / Shutterstock.com, multiple interior pages

45th Parallel Press is an imprint of Cherry Lake Publishing.

Library of Congress Cataloging-in-Publication Data

Loh-Hagan, Virginia.
  Sound effects artist / Virginia Loh-Hagan.
      pages cm — (odd jobs)
  Includes bibliographical references and index.
  ISBN 978-1-63470-029-0 (hardcover) — ISBN 978-1-63470-083-2 (pdf) — ISBN 978-1-63470-056-6
(pbk.) — ISBN 978-1-63470-110-5 (ebook)
1. Motion pictures—Sound effects—Juvenile literature. 2. Animated films—Sound effects—Juvenile
literature. 3. Video games—Sound effects—Juvenile literature. I. Title.

  TK7881.4.L575 2015
  777'.53023—dc23

                           2015008291

Cherry Lake Publishing would like to acknowledge the work of The Partnership for 21st Century Skills.
Please visit www.p21.org for more information.

Printed in the United States of America
Corporate Graphics Inc.

Contents

CHAPTER 1

Hearing is Believing

What do sound effects artists make sounds for? How do sound effects artists tell stories? How do sound effects artists make things feel real? When are sound effects added to movies?

Caoimhe Doyle makes sounds for movies and TV shows. She worked on a scene. Characters were having a sword fight. She made sounds of the swords moving. She made the swords sound fast and heavy. She made the sound of the characters moving.

Sound effects **enhance** stories. Enhance means to make something better. They shouldn't **distract** from the stories. Distract means to take your attention away. Doyle said, "The picture will tell you what is going on. But sound tells you how to feel about what is going on."

Sound effects artists tell stories. They help make shows feel more real.

Sound effects artists work on movies and television shows.

Tchae Measroch makes sounds for video games. He splashes in a bathtub. He taps on a bear skull. He matches what's in the game with sound. He wants players to believe the action. Sound effects make the game feel real.

Video games can take place in fantasy worlds. Measroch invents sounds for noises he's never heard. He made the sound of a pirate falling on a ship's deck. He used a leather purse with metal rings. He hit it against wood.

He loves his odd job. He said, "It's like being the stuntman of sound."

Sound effects artists work on video games and phone apps.

THAT HAPPENED?!?

Monique Reymond worked on reality TV shows. She made sounds of people eating weird things. They ate things like stomach guts. She made sounds for people doing weird things. People were in a fish tank full of roaches. She said, "All of that stuff does not really have a sound associated with it. We put that in. At first, when I started *Fear Factor*, I was very creeped out by the content. And then what I grew to realize is it was one of the most creative things that I'd ever gotten to do." She made worms sound different from roaches. She made different chewing sounds. She has to be creative. She said, "Trying to figure out how to make a wide range of sounds working with very little is, I think, a great part of the creativity."

Curtis Takahashi makes sounds for the Seattle Radio Theater. They produce live radio shows. Actors read lines on the radio.

He makes the radio shows feel real. He enhances the drama. He enhances the humor. He makes sound effects to match what the actors say. He works alongside the actors. He works on live shows. So he can't make mistakes.

Sound effects artists work on radio shows and commercials.

Sound effects artists want viewers to believe in the scene. They make sounds to match the actions of each scene. They also create **ambience**. Ambience is background noise. It's water dripping in the sink. It's dogs barking in the street.

People are used to hearing noises. They notice when sounds are missing. Sound effects artists make sure that sounds fit in to the scene.

Sound effects are added to movies **postproduction**. That means after the movie is filmed. This helps actors. Filming sounds can be distracting. Actors might miss their lines. Sound effects artists help actors focus.

Sound effects artists work in the background.

Being a Foley Artist

Who is Jack Donovan Foley? What is a Foley artist? What is a Foley stage? How are Foley artists and sound effects artists the same and different?

Jack Donovan Foley developed many sound effects **techniques**. Techniques are tips or methods. He invented the process of adding sound effects. He made special sounds for special scenes. Sound effects artists are sometimes called "Foley artists."

Early cameras did not record footsteps well. Foley

copied how famous actors walked. He invented Foley walking. Foley watched movies on a screen. He made the sound of footsteps. The timing had to be perfect. The sounds and actions had to match.

Sound effects artists work on **locations** or in soundproof studios.

Foley artists work on a Foley stage. The stage has **pits**. A pit is a hole. Each pit has a different floor. Dirt, gravel, wood, marble, and concrete cover these floors. The stage also has **props**. Props are objects used to make sounds.

Foley made sounds for a large Roman army. Soldiers were fighting with metal shields and swords. He jingled keys in front of the **microphone**. The microphone is a tool that picks up sound.

Sound design has three main parts: music, voices, and noises.

Spotlight Biography
MICHAEL WINSLOW

Michael Winslow is known as the "Man of 10,000 Sound Effects." He can make more than 1,000 sound effects using his voice. He can sound like barking dogs. He can sound like squishy sneakers. He grew up on Air Force bases. He used to copy airplane sounds. He performed at comedy clubs. He's acted in hit comedy movies. He's provided voices and sounds for movies, TV shows, theme park rides, phone apps, video games, and commercials.

Sound effects artists and Foley artists both make sounds. But they are different. Sound effects artists work on all types of sounds. Like explosions and car doors slamming. Foley artists make the actions and movements of people.

Sound effects artists work on live shows and recorded shows. Foley artists work on recorded shows. They make sounds postproduction.

CHAPTER 3

Different Types of Sounds

What are the three main groups of Foley effects? What are hard sound effects? What are background sound effects? What are sound design effects?

"Foley effects" are three main groups of sounds. They are: feet, cloth, and props.

Foley artists spend a lot of time making footsteps. They follow characters in the show. They copy their moves. They run. They walk. They jump. Jeff Wilhoit and Jim Moriana are Foley walkers. They have more than 100 pairs of shoes.

Foley artists make the sounds of clothes. Clothes move as people walk. Pant legs rub together. Foley artists rub two pieces of material together. They do this near the microphone.

Foley artists make the sounds of actors using props. People make sounds as they open doors. People make sounds as they use phones. Foley artists make sure movies sound real.

People make a lot of sounds. Foley artists work hard to capture each one.

17

Sound Effects Artist
KNOW THE LINGO!

Boom: a long pole that projects the microphone over the set

Cue sheet: time codes for the beginning and ending of any action and a description of the action that helps the film editors know where the sound goes

Designed FX: sounds made for things that don't exist in our world

FX: effects (say "ef-fects")

Hard FX: sounds of on-screen world objects such as cars, crashes, doors, phone sounds, sirens, etc.

Loose mic'd: placing the mic 6 to 10 feet (2 to 3 meters) from the sound source

Mic: short for microphone

Soundscape: sounds that define a specific period, location, or feeling

Sweetening: fine-tuning the sound in postproduction

Tight mic'd: placing the mic 3 feet (1 m) or less away from the sound source

Walla: background sound effects that are added to make an ambiance outside of the frame of action

Walla group: a group of actors who provide background conversation that looks real. Actors say "walla walla" over and over so they look like they're having a real conversation

There are four other categories of sound effects.

Hard sound effects are common sounds. They are door alarms, gunshots, punches, and cars driving by.

Background sound effects are part of the ambience. They give setting. They are forest sounds. They are people talking in a restaurant. They are bird sounds.

Electronic sound effects are made by a keyboard. They are laser blasts and spaceship hums. They are popular in science-fiction movies and video games.

Sound design effects are sounds of unreal objects. This means monsters and aliens. They are sounds of things you can't recreate. Like the sounds of ships sinking.

Sound effects artists make all kinds of sounds.

CHAPTER 4

Wanting to Make Sounds

How did John Roesch become a sound effects artist? How do sound effects artists learn to be sound effects artists? What are some tips to being a sound effects artist?

John Roesch has worked on more than 400 projects. He helped a friend make sounds for a movie. He did a lot of running. He was good as a Foley artist. He thought it was a "silly job."

He met his neighbor. She was a Foley artist.

He said, "Four days later, I got hired at the company where she worked and I never looked back."

Sound effects artists are like composers. They put together different sounds.

Roesch said, "Foley looks easy but to really be a master at the craft is extremely difficult. … The first 10 years were tough. I got lucky and got with people where I learned a lot." Many sound effects artists get inspired. They work with other artists.

Advice From the Field
BEN BURTT

Ben Burtt is famous for making sound effects for *Star Wars* and the Indiana Jones movies. He studies sounds. He said, "I would study the gunshots in all the movies that I loved. And I'd ask, 'How did they do it?'" He goes on trips to collect sounds. He made sounds for a cart chase in a mine. He needed sounds of carts going down tracks and around corners. So his team rode roller coasters at Disneyland. They did this at night when the park was closed. Burtt uses whatever he can find. One time, he needed sounds of falling rocks and buildings. His team carried rocks and gravel up a hill. They pushed them down the hill. Sound effects artists think every location can be a recording studio.

Sounds are everywhere. Sound effects artists collect sounds.

Sound effects artists learn from other artists. Many sound effects artists start as assistants. They learn to use the equipment. They collect sounds. They **experiment** with sounds. Experiment means to play with and test.

Jack Stew says, "Listen to sounds. If a ruler sounds interesting, keep boinging it. Or squeeze a bottle. You build this whole sound bank in your head."

CHAPTER 5

Challenges and Creativity

What are some challenges faced by sound effects artists? In what ways do sound effects artists show their creativity?

There are challenges to being a sound effects artist. Alyson Dee Moore said, "You are really on your feet all day. … It's tough on your body."

Making sound effects is the last step. This means sound effects artists must work fast.

Sound effects artists must invent new sounds.

Gary Rydstrom made sounds for dinosaurs. No one knows what dinosaurs sound like. He recorded animal sounds. He recorded his friend growling. He recorded himself breathing into a tube. He put them together.

Rydstrom uses his pets to make sounds. Noises from his dog Buster became T-rex sounds. He recorded Buster eating. That sound was used in a robot fight scene.

Technology has improved sound effects.

WHEN ODD IS TOO ODD!

Alex Joseph is a sound effects artist. He works hard to make the perfect sounds. He made the sound of a head being chopped off. Most sound effects artists use watermelons or cabbages. Joseph used green coconuts. They're covered with stringy fiber. He said, "It sounds just like a human head." Joseph also made sounds for a chocolate river. He jumped into a pool. He filled the pool with a powder. The powder made a jelly. He wanted the river to sound thick. He said, "I was swimming about in the stuff all day. But it was very gloopy. I had to take four showers to get it all off." He made the sounds for the floating books in *Harry Potter*. He bought many old books. He said, "A newer book just wouldn't have made the same sound."

Ben Burtt also used sounds from his pets. He worked on *Star Wars*. He made the sound for a beast. He used his dog. He slowed the barks down.

Burtt also puts sounds together. He made the sound of a light **saber**. A saber is a sword. He used the hum of a projector. He used the buzz from an old TV. He put them together.

Working on historical movies is hard. Sound effects artists can't use today's sounds. Frank Warner travels. He finds the right sounds. He worked on a western movie. He went to Utah and Montana.

Sound effects artists make sure sounds are true to history.

Sound effects artists use props to make sounds.

Marko Costanzo has made sound effects for more than 469 projects. He made the sound of galloping horses. He used coconut shells. They were stuffed with cloth or rocks. He made the sound of walking dogs. He used gloves with nails.

Costanzo carries props with him. They are always packed in his SUV. He has celery and eggshells. These sound like broken bones. He has a wooden block. This sounds like old buildings.

Sometimes, he makes footsteps for women. His most interesting props are large women's shoes. They fit him. He said that's "not an easy thing to find."

DID YOU KNOW?

- Samurai films are Japanese movies about warriors. The actors use swords. Sound effects artists make the sound of swords cutting into human flesh. They stick chopsticks into dead chickens.

- Mistakes happen. *How the Grinch Stole Christmas* is a movie. Cindy Lou Who goes to the Grinch's house for first time. She knocks on the door. The sound is not synced with the action. In the middle of *The Hobbit: The Battle of the Five Armies*, a sword fell to the ground. It makes no sound.

- *Finding Nemo* is a movie. Gary Rydstrom worked on the sound effects. He made the sound of moving ocean water. He used a hot tub, a fish tank, and the ocean. He made the sound of the two main characters bouncing off jellyfish. He flicked his finger on a hot water bottle. The dentist's drill was recorded when someone on his team went to the dentist.

- Slot machines are games at casinos. People put coins in the machine. They pull the lever, or handle. They hope to win big. These machines make many jingling sounds. Casinos use sound effects. They want people to keep playing. The sounds make people think they're winning. This means people spend more money.

- There's a Guinness World Record for the quietest place on Earth. It's a room at the Orfield Laboratories in Minnesota. It's called an anechoic chamber. Anechoic means free from echo. The room has concrete walls 1 foot (30.5 centimeters) thick. The room absorbs 99.99 percent of all sound. Nobody has lasted more than 45 minutes in this room. When it's too quiet, human brains focus on sounds inside the body. They hear heartbeats, flowing blood, organs, and breathing. It drives people crazy.

- Gregg Barbanell made the sound of victims falling to the floor. He hit a boxing glove against his own body.

- Sound effects artists make sounds for fight scenes. Ben Burtt uses pumpkins. He puts a croquet ball in a sock. He beats a pumpkin with it. He said this produces a "meaty, kind of choppy sound."

CONSIDER THIS!

TAKE A POSITION! It takes many people to make a movie. Actors and directors usually get all the credit. Sound effects artists are usually unknown to the public. Do you think they should be recognized by viewers? Why or why not? Argue your position with reasons and evidence.

SAY WHAT? Some people think sound effects artists and Foley artists are the same thing. Some people think sound effects artists and Foley artists are different. Explain how they are similar and how they are different.

THINK ABOUT IT! Sound effects artists use ordinary objects to make sounds. For example, a car crash is made by breaking drinking glasses. A breaking bone is made by snapping celery. Think about movie sounds. How would you make various sounds using objects from your house?

SEE A DIFFERENT SIDE! Some people think sound effects artists will lose their jobs. They think computers will take over. Making sounds on computers is cheaper than hiring sound effects artists. Sound effects artists argue that their job is special. They think real sound effects are better than digital sound effects. They make art. Sandy Buchanan said, "The real sound of a bone breaking would be quite boring. … But the sound of celery snapping, designed, produced, and engineered by a professional, can be stomach-churning." What do you think?

LEARN MORE

PRIMARY SOURCES
"Northvale Foley Artists Add Effects": http://video.pbs.org/video/2365313884/
"Sound Advice: An Interview with Ben Burtt": www.starwars.com/video/sound-advice-an-interview-with-ben-burtt

SECONDARY SOURCES
Horn, Geoffrey M. *Movie Soundtracks and Sound Effects.* Milwaukee, WI: Gareth Stevens Publishing, 2007.
McMullin, Dan Taulapapa. *Lights, Camera, Action!* Huntington Beach, CA: Creative Teaching Press, 2009.
Platt, Richard. *Film.* New York: DK Eyewitness Books, 2000.

WEB SITES
Association of Sound Designers: www.theasd.uk/#abouthome
Cinema Audio Society: http://cinemaaudiosociety.org
Motion Picture Association of America: www.mpaa.org

GLOSSARY

ambience (AM-bee-ehns) background noise, atmosphere

distract (di-STRAKT) to pull attention away from something

enhance (en-HANS) to make something bigger or better

experiment (ik-SPER-uh-ment) to test or play around with

microphone (MYE-kruh-fone) a tool that picks up sound

pits (PITS) boxes in a Foley stage made of various flooring materials

postproduction (pohst-pruh-DUHK-shuhn) after filming

props (PRAHPS) objects used to make sounds

saber (SAY-bur) sword

techniques (tek-NEEKS) tips or methods

INDEX

ABOUT THE AUTHOR

Dr. Virginia Loh-Hagan is an author, university professor, former classroom teacher, and curriculum designer. She loves movies, music, and sounds. She lives in San Diego with her very tall husband and very naughty dogs. To learn more about her, visit www.virginialoh.com.